Praise for
wild life

"Each morning, I treat myself to a poem by Jamie K. Reaser. Thoughtful, evocative, and welling up from a deeply sacred place, her words are my morning meditation, my morning prayer. Although *Wild Life* is bundled as a book of poetry, I know it to be what it truly is: Spiritual practice. Thank you, Jamie, for such a gift."
—Susan Chernak McElroy, author of *Animals as Teachers and Healers* and *Why Buffalo Dance*

"In *Wild Life*, Jamie K. Reaser offers a wonderful cascade of stories, a flurry of images and imaginings, that each reconnect us to ourselves while weaving us boldly into the fragile and extravagant wildness of life. From the immensity of the bear to the morning quiver of hermit thrushes, *Wild Life* shares a wisdom of watching and learning in, and with, the wild."
—Sean Southey, Executive Director, PCI Media Impact

"I am taken back by the brilliance of Jamie K. Reaser's poetry. She draws you into the wilds of the land and her heart and deep wisdom steps out to take you home every time. Her love of the natural world and weavings of spiritual truth are akin to Mary Oliver. Thank you, Jamie, for the superlative gift of your poetry."
—Mare Cromwell, author of *Messages from Mother . . . . Earth Mother*

ALSO BY JAMIE K REASER

Courting the Wild: Love Affairs with Reptiles and Amphibians · 2009
Huntley Meadows: A Naturalist's Journal in Verse · 2010
Note to Self: Poems for Changing the World from the Inside Out · 2011
Sacred Reciprocity: Courting the Beloved in Everyday Life · 2012

with Susan Chernak McElroy
Courting the Wild: Love Affairs with the Land · 2008

wild life

NEW AND SELECTED POEMS

JAMIE K REASER

with a foreword by Edward E. Clark, Jr.

HIRAETH PRESS
DANVERS, MASSACHUSETTS

Cover photographs
Bear fur © Anton Derevschuk/Shutterstock.com
All other photos © Jamie K. Reaser
Cover and text design by Jason Kirkey

ISBN: 978-0-9889430-0-1
First Edition 2012

Hiraeth Press books may be purchased for education, business or sale promotional use. For information, please write:
Special Markets
Hiraeth Press
P.O. Box 1442
Pawcatuck, CT 06379-1968

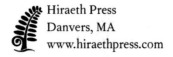

Hiraeth Press
Danvers, MA
www.hiraethpress.com

This book is for those
dedicated to keeping
the wild alive

THE INHERITANCE

I open the door to the world every morning,
anticipating, wondering
who will be the first to greet me
as I step onto the earth
with eyes still soft from dreaming.

Will it be pine, or pine warbler?

Who will be beside me when
I kneel at the pond,
walk through the wood,
cross the meadow?
Will I notice them?
Will they notice me?
Never are my days lived alone.
Never are my breaths less than
an exchange of breaths
with some other soul.
Everything wants to be known.
So, for awhile each day, I tend to this
mutual desire for belonging,

Saying, "Hello pretty girl," to the doe,
stroking the pussy willows,
meditating beside a frog.
This is how I apprentice to love
and learn to speak those forgotten words
that acknowledge every living thing
as a simple miracle.

When the day comes that my body
no longer needs to walk out the door
in order to know this fine world,

I pray that some young person is
stepping across their threshold,

taking a deep breath in the morning air,
and realizing,
this is my inheritance.

CONTENTS

xi · Foreword
xiii · Introduction

LISTENING TO THE WILD

3 · The African Elephant
7 · The Armadillo
10 · Bear Medicine
13 · Blue Feathers
15 · Cicadas
17 · Courting the Viper
19 · Doe, A Deer
23 · Falling From Grace
24 · The Feast
27 · Finally, I Get It
28 · Home is Here
30 · The Hook
33 · The Jaguar's Bite
36 · The Message ('Buddy's Poem')
38 · The Opossum in the Road
45 · Turtles
46 · The Vow

FREEING THE WILD

51 · At the Heart of the Meadow
53 · Beetles
55 · Break Free
56 · Akhilandeshavari's Crocodile
59 · The Crayfish
61 · Emergence
64 · Hermit Thrushes in the Morning
66 · The Insistent Moth
68 · The Mark
71 · Meangingful Relationship
73 · The Nightingale
78 · The Oriole by the River
80 · A Rabbit in the Porch Light

82 · Soul Lines

84 · Subtle Beauty

88 · Whooo

92 · The Winter Wren

LIVING WILD

97 · Answers for Mary

98 · The Eaglet

100 · Eastern Bluebirds and Purple Spiderworts

104 · Fawn

105 · Finches in the Morning

107 · Freeze and Thaw

109 · In This Way

112 · Irrational Optimism

114 · Owl

115 · Red Fox

116 · Rising

117 · Sacraments

119 · Song for the Reindeer

121 · Swerving to Miss Caterpillars

122 · Tadpoles in Tire Rut

123 · The Vittles of Death

126 · A Walking Stick Sighting

127 · What is Joy to the Snapping Turtle?

129 · The Woodpecker

131 · Acknowledgments

132 · About The Wildlife Center Of Virginia

133 · About The Author

Foreword

W hen I was first asked to write the foreword for this book, I confess that the request was greeted with something less than enthusiasm. Basically, I don't read poetry. Still, Jamie K. Reaser has been a close friend, valued colleague, and volunteer for the Wildlife Center of Virginia for 30 years. We first met when Jamie was 15. If there is one thing I have learned in the last three decades, it is that Jamie is not a person to whom it is easy to say *no*!

So, finally, on a chilly spring morning in early May, I braced myself, sat down at the base of a big oak tree near my cabin in the mountains, and turned the first page. What I never expected was that I would not stop turning pages for the next three hours, until each and every word in this book had been read, pondered, re-read, and savored. This is actually the first book of poetry I have ever managed to read all the way through; and, I am looking forward to doing it again in the near future!

So, what makes this book so special?

That is a challenging question.

For me, I suppose it is because this book enables the reader to examine their relationship with the natural world . . . in fact, one's relationship with the *spirit* of the natural world. While I cherish my personal engagement with nature, and have actually made a career out of defending, conserving and restoring wild things and wild places, it was the exploration of the spiritual aspects of this engagement that was so compelling. What was so unnerving is that this book seems to have been written specifically to enable me to contemplate things I usually go out of my way to *avoid* considering . . . little things . . . like *the meaning of life*!

I'm a guy who feels that I was somehow set upon a path in life; and while I don't always know where the path leads, I have spent my entire life racing along. This book not only gives me clues about *where* the path may lead, but *why* I am so compelled to keep moving forward. Maybe I am not that different from a salmon or a migrating bird. I certainly did not expect to find such insight in a book, and certainly not in a collection of poems.

Part of my inability to actually consider many of life's important questions is the difficultly of reducing such cosmic questions to words, let alone putting them on the printed page. Make no mistake about it, I'm a man of many words, and I communicate for a living, but I am astonished at how *these* words say things I could never say, and convey concepts I could never articulate.

There are many clichés about "communing with nature" or being a "tree hugger." After reading *Wild Life*, those phrases seem less cliché than profound. I suppose until you have truly communed with nature, or experienced the energy that can come from hugging a tree, you can't appreciate how powerful such experiences can be. The ability to tap into nature on such a spiritual level is not something you just do; it is something you must gradually learn. The hard part is finding a teacher.

Jamie K. Reaser is such a teacher, and *Wild Life* is her textbook. Each reader will take away something different from this work, but I promise you that whatever it is, it will be powerful and it will be extremely personal. You will reflect on things about which you may never have thought. You will feel things you may never have experienced. And, you will look at the natural world around you – and your impact upon it – in a new way.

I did not expect all this. I probably was not prepared for all of this. But I could not stop reading *Wild Life*. I commend this work to anyone who cares about the natural world. It is essential reading for those who wish to have a deeper and more meaningful relationship with that world.

On behalf of the Wildlife Center of Virginia, the animals for which we care, and the humans whose lives we touch, I want to thank Jamie and her publisher for dedicating a portion of the proceeds from this book to supporting the Wildlife Center's life-saving and life-changing work. Even though I initially considered a book of poetry to be a pretty far-fetched project for us to support and promote, I now recognize that this little book will be a very valuable tool for the Wildlife Center, as we advance our mission of *teaching the world to care about, and care for, wildlife and the environment.*

—Edward E. Clark, Jr.
President
The Wildlife Center of Virginia

Introduction

I was six years old when I consciously dedicated my life to wildlife conservation. Mentors encouraged me to secure strong academic credentials in biology and build a career that would influence environmental decision making on a global scale. I did these things.

I did these things and discovered along the way that wildlife conservation cannot be achieved unless the primary focus of our efforts is on fostering and protecting the wild nature of the human animal.

The human psyche's relationship to the wild – a force often feared within and around us – is the basis of our relationship with the natural world. Looking around us, we can see evidence of our perceived need to keep the wild at bay...destruction and domestication.

This collection of poems is a reflection of my personal journey to befriend the wild, to apprentice to it, to increasingly become a creature of it. This is, yes, a spiritual quest. The poetry emerges out of a deep conversation with the soul – the primal self.

Ultimately, *Wild Life: New and Selected Poems* is meant to be a testament to what becomes possible when we see ourselves as a part of, rather than apart from, Nature.

What can an owl, a salmon, or a bear teach us about becoming a better person?

What if we re-claimed our animalness?

What if we surrendered to the wild life?

What then becomes possible for wild nature in all its forms?

Perhaps, everything.

—Jamie K. Reaser
Blue Ridge Mountains
Virginia

LISTENING TO THE WILD

THE AFRICAN ELEPHANT

There is no recourse but to pause
and gasp, besieged by wonderment,
when you realize this love-challenged world
of ours, still,
still,
is holding space for such
raw and aged magnificence.

I couldn't have dreamed him,
not even if I were the most gifted
of dreamers –

Dreams are humble enough to know
when they are best left in
in a pillow's shallow cup.

He's what makes reality
worth visiting.

And, in this moment,

sigh,

if Amboseli offered to write
my name in her salty dust,
I might be inclined to stay
for awhile . . .

Barefoot,

A woman remembering
what it really means
to be wild.

A maiden in the bush.

I've met elders before;

Their palms are so worn from
story telling with their hands
that their lifelines take up residence
in their eyes.

This one too.

And on his hide,
the intersecting
valleys and ridges
of a thousand parched wrinkles
collect in drapes and folds
at belly and ankle.

In concentric circles they cascade down
the length of his long, thick trunk
to its sensitive tip -
where he explores and reasons
unreasonable things.

These places that generations
of red-billed oxpeckers
have used as perches and swing sets,
gravity employs to record time,

and wisdom earned.

He understands what a day is for.

Perhaps this savannah
wouldn't be so dry

if we all understood.
Sometimes the vervets climb
into the acacias and tell
his story.

He collects their gossip in the
flap of his ears and lets it
bounce a bit.

Sometimes it comes closer to
the truth that way.

None of them were there
to see.

For them, the horizon lines
have always been a place
of emptiness.

He re-members herds so large
the earth was a bed of rolling,
hoof-thundering clouds.

This is what gave the Maasai their
sense of rhythm and inspired
them to take joyous leaps of faith.

This was before the free ones
were called "game."
Before there was a price tag on
his tusks.
Before he wondered if his last
breath would be seized by bullets
and saw blades.

Certainly,
This would disappoint
the dung beetles,

he muses.

Still, being loyal to ghosts
is a wearisome task
for the yet-living.

How do I convince an elephant
that we can learn?

Might he be inspired to hope?

If I asked,

Could he tell me where we went wrong?

THE ARMADILLO

Even the armadillo,
tucked within his banded armor,
maintains a soft underbelly.

It is possible for you to say, "No!"
while holding love
in your heart -

Love for yourSelf,
and love for Other.

Unconditional love,
does not equal
unconditional relationship.

Your boundaries are there
to hold you in a blessed
embrace,

To wrap around that which
is so worthy of protection.

To be a medicine blanket.

There is a reason that "No!"
was one of the first words
your child-mouth uttered:

You are precious,

And that little one of you knew it,
knew it like breath,
knew it like giggles,

knew it like the wonderment
of every first.

Knew it in the kicks and screams,
tears and flush red face
when something just
wasn't right.

I wish that I could have been
there that moment,
that fragile decisive moment,
when someone convinced
you that you weren't
good anymore.

Not good.

Not good enough.

Not good.
Not worthy.
Not worthy enough
for,

"No!"

But I wasn't there.

No true adult was;

Somewhere along the way
the initiation rites
were wronged.

So,

Now we must listen
ever so carefully
to the elders:

The armadillo says,

"Let love be your softness."

"Let love,

 be your softness."

Take a leap of faith:
Love yourself and
our collective future
enough to say, "No!"

to everyone and everything
that violates the soul.

BEAR MEDICINE

I saw you there in the
humid oak-poplar wood
of late summer morning.

Lanky young bruin
with perfect posture
and amble,

deftly trampling the
delicate ostrich ferns
with each
magnificent
pawfall
as you made your
way, intentfully
and agape,
up the rocky mountain slope.

I waited,

patiently,

like someone who had
just found an unyielding
faith in long-rumored miracles.

Your journey and my journey
will intersect this day.

"Bear medicine,"
some would say.

And we did have our moment.

Yes.

Standing still.

Fully aware of the other's earthly presence.

Looking deeply into each other's sight-full eyes.

Breathing each other's privileged breath
in a way that even a poet shouldn't
try to explain.

And, there, on sacred ground,
I couldn't contemplate "bear medicine."

Couldn't feel it tingling the hairs on my arms.

Couldn't sense it transforming the course of my days.

Couldn't bring myself to walk,
for even a second,
between the thin-veiled worlds.

No, no as we moved on from that moment,

You climbing Northwest,
Me climbing Southwest,

All I could think about was this:

What is human medicine to a bear?

What is human medicine to a bear?

Is it powerful?

Is it kind?

Does it leave you feeling grateful and graced?

Or, is it...?

Or, does it...?

This is what you left me with.

This question:

What is human medicine to a bear?

This question.

This question that has stilled me
in the dark silence of mySelf,

seeking the wisdom of thoughts
I've never before known.

Yes.

Yes.

Bear medicine.

BLUE FEATHERS

Holding ever so tentatively the blue jay feather
in the casual stream of afternoon sunlight,
I turn it back and forth
contemplating Truth.

No pigment,
only what eye and brain
conspire to See.

Blue.

Not at all blue.

What else is boldly portraying itself
with confident illusion?

Tucking the feather behind my
right ear
draws out the impish, giggling
little tom girl of me.

Oh how she loves to play
with feathers!

And I watch her there
sitting on grass,
twirling plumes in feral rays

and I begin to count
the culturally-refracted fallacies that
she has been bottle fed:

"Silence is rewarded."

"Boys are more important."

"Normalcy is a requisite for love."

"Profit should trump passion."

"You can only love one."

When did we all stop suckling
on the nipple of Authenticity?
Why were our rattles taken away
before we could fully embody
our own unique rhythm
into the world?

How come we learned to scream
"No! No! No!"
before being invited to play
in the joy bubbles of
"YES! YES! YES!" . . . ?

I join her on the manicured lawn,
letting my clothed buttocks settle onto
ground that once had a different
perspective on what it was right to grow.

Drawing her into my lap with a smile
and nurturing embrace,

I whisper The Secret of Life into her left ear:

"Hold your beliefs loosely,

and always test them in the Light."

Blue jay feathers do not contain blue pigment. The impression of blue color
results from the brain/eye processing of light refracted from the feathers.

CICADAS

The curanderos have shed
their last underworldly skin
and taken to the trees.

Chakapa wings drone icaros,
incanting me into my
animal nature
and beyond all hope
of aloneness.

Since my very first summer,
this has been
what a million essential insects
have asked of me.

Today I heard them.

~

When I was a young girl
I'd pluck cicada exoskeletons
off tree trunks and fence posts.

Bronze and sun-crisped,
I'd delight in the concept that
form can be outgrown.

I adorned my ear lobes with them,
and my fingers –
Like priceless jewels,
the riches of the wooed and betrothed.

Little then did I know
that it was this child's play

that would teach me
how to fall in love.

~

I said, "Yes!"
and became a bride
to the world.

COURTING THE VIPER

Baba Gulabgir I pray to you:
teach me the magic
of the serpent pot.

The vipers they rise
swaying with lies and manipulations
on muscular stalk,
fastening cold black eyes
on me.

Practiced strikes land upon my flesh
and eat into my soul.

Necroses and bloodletting
commence
as scarlet
pairs of liquid beads -

Droplets of my precious
personed being.

The Wounded One screams
in pain as the toxins circulate
and madden.

Though sitting on my cushion,
I am unsettled by rage
and visions
of retaliatory get-evenings.

Will the body still
writhe when severed
from the head?

I struggle to find my way
out of conflict with
integrity —
but like a rodent that is
already halfway down
the elongated stomach.

No.

I cannot, will not,
embrace a peace
that is declared
by my willing victimhood.

Patiently waiting for me to finally
take a breath,

the Guru gently says:

"Lift your flute.

Play.

Court the venomous snakes
with Life's most
rapturous music.

Dear One,

It is the alchemy of love
that transforms poison
into medicine."

DOE, A DEER

Doe, a deer,
a female deer
standing in ironic be-wild-er-ment
amidst a still-screaming clear cut.

Have you seen
the big yellow monster
that destroyed her home?

Blades that have never known
the ethics of a Ninja.

She now has PTSD
and is too numb
to grieve,
to dash,
to join the stumps in their collective shrieks
of amputation.

My eyes catch a glimpse
of a single flower that made it through –
Podophyllum peltatum –
Mayapple.

Eternal hope.

I'll ask you again:

"Have you seen
the big yellow monster
that destroyed her home?"

It dwells within you,
you know.

The Destroyer –
That part of you that takes more
than you need.
That takes everything you need.

Look! She's moving,
shifting her head so that
her big brown watery eyes meet your eyes.

She can See that you are human,

but she just doesn't get it.

And neither do you –

And neither do I –

despite the long practiced walk and talk.

How is it that even those of us
who have awakened to the consequences of
our actions still largely
partake in hypocrisy?

It's all about the fuel that goes into
the Big Yellow Monster
of You
and Me:

Insecurity,
Fear,
Loneliness...

These things drive the harvest rates
of that which is Beautiful –

both within us
and outside us.

So, it is time All,
that we call for an alternative energy source:

Compassion,
Love,
Unity...

We start not by monkey-wrenching
The Destroyer,
but by bringing The Destroyer into
ecstatic relationship with The Creator.

I'll say it again:

"We start not by monkey-wrenching
The Destroyer,
but by bringing The Destroyer into
ecstatic relationship with The Creator."

Her udder is becoming painful
as it swells,
and there will be no relief.

The twins were dismembered
and disemboweled
as they did what ancestral memory
told them to do –
place your lovely white spots
in the glitter of leaf-sieved sunlight
and be still.

Two Mothers will mourn
and someone else
will refer to these and other casualties
simply as "negative externalities"
of Progress.

Look within.
Go within.
Redefine Progress
for youSelf and
for our species
before you fuel your
next outward step.

FALLING FROM GRACE

Where I sat on the crumbling brick wall
the pigeon fell,
gasping its last two breaths in my lap
while our eyes introduced our souls.

When I looked to heavens above,
there was only sky, cobalt blue.

What were the chances?

I know what it is to fall from grace -

That rocket-shot tumble
facilitated by your own dead weight
thundering the surface identity into
a direct collision course with
the very foundation of Life.

The impact is the point.

So many times, I've missed it.

Sigh.

It took a poisoned pigeon
to teach me this:

"Rest your weary wings
and unfold your heart
on the way down."

It's the only way
to land with Grace.

THE FEAST

I am here, wondering about the
worth of my days
to your stew pot and virulence.

I knew every cadence of the river.
Every color of the flowing sky.
The meandering of the heavens.
And below – smells and textures –
silt and loam and plant.

You could have come
and asked me of these things.

You would have learned:

This is the intimacy that makes a man.

The wisdom of millennia has taught me
that the body must become a testament to listening;

Life is conversation.
Living is ceremony.

So, I ask you:

What is this emptiness you seek to feed?

In your gut, you do know.

Hollowness.

So,

Look now

upon the empty,
gutless shell of a being
in your hand.

That was me.

That is you.

I can assure you, this is not the way
to satiate hungry ghosts.

We sit together at the same table,
you and I,
and the haunting pain of separation.

We partake of the same destiny.

"Come. Follow me," invites the river.

"Come. Open to me," invites the sky.

"Come. Pray with me," invites the heavens.

"Come. Let's touch each other," invites all the others.

Do you hear it?

Everything.

Everything,

is inviting you into relationship.

You are here on the bank of the river,

We are all here basking on the bank of the river,

to learn

to feast

upon

the heart.

FINALLY, I GET IT

I keep trying to speak eloquently
on behalf
of an eagle,

Pushing at words,

And failing,
miserably.

He says,

"Where there is power,

there is no
need
for force."

HOME IS HERE

In the black walnuts, newly leafing, warblers flit
and swish about, testing the age of my ear
and long-term memory. American redstart, northern parula,
yellow-rumped. Oh, and there's a blue-grey
gnatchatcher scit-scatting. Wiggle, left, right, left, right.
I wonder: What is this place to them? Do they have a name for it?

Home? Not home?

On that day when they all decide to come northward,
does one of them suddenly chip, "Let's go home!" Or, is that
something they sing in sonnet form before heading South?

If only I was more fluent in little bird languages.

After considerable pondering,

I decide these might be migratory bodhisattvas:
beings who have learned to live exquisitely in the moment.
Home is here. Home is there. It's a nest, a branch,
a piece of sky – with or without clouds. Maybe
it's the edge of a stream when taking a drink or a bath, or
a ceramic vessel that some kind soul placed in their garden
because they love brightly colored things that fly and give
sweet verse.

Maybe I am overthinking this.

Cerulean. Worm-eating. Black-throated green.

Naughty cowbird.

Here. In this tree. For a moment.

Maybe I could be present too.

Totally.

Home.

THE HOOK

You are a largemouth bass,
Micropertus salmoides,
gulping water and ushering
it passed your feathery gills,

focusing your steely,
golden eyes on that which
is just inches from your
well-practiced jowls,

undulating your dorsal fin
and tail just enough to
keep your densely scaled, robust body
suspended in the water column

so that you can decide.

The thick, ruddy
night-crawler-of-a-worm
thrashes there before you,
twisting and turning in such a manner
that your neurotransmitters can do little
more than concoct the invitation
"Eat me!"

"Eat me!" –
as if the Universe has suddenly decided
to offer up to you the winning
gastronomic lottery ticket.

You could bite,

or you could look more closely.

Here's what I see –

A *Lugumbricus terrestris*
in sheer agony:
impaled,
folded,
and impaled again and again,
drowning.

The metallic barbed hook
is secured to a clear nylon line
studded with three lead sinkers.

Eight feet up a plastic red-and-white bobber
is riding the lake's breeze waves,
waiting, eagerly
to be the spokesperson
of your demise.

The line continues on to a rod,
and then into a reel.

The ready hands on grip
are your own.

Your own.

So, what's it going to be?

What is your karmic decision?
Are you going to get hooked
by the Old Patterns that
no longer serve you,
and perhaps never did?

Or, are you going to
seek and earn
authentic nourishment
elsewhere?

I pray that you don't let
Self-deception and
instant gratification
be the utensils of your
last supper.

THE JAGUAR'S BITE

The jaguar gripped my hand
in his wet and gnashing mouth.

Wounds are mysterious things;

How they can speak out so long
and loud
after new skin and new stories
tuck them
out of sight...

Sometimes it's hard to put a
name to the old voice,

Mostly because there are so
many options:

Shame, grief, despair, anger, rage,
Fear...

But it is a growl that is recognizable –

in the ear of memory,
or the pit of the stomach.

And, in the last breath of an addict,
the jingle of prison cell keys,
the door slamming on bruised and beaten hearts,
the moment that innocence is stolen.

And, in all the Self-betrayals.

In every act of prey turned predator.

Unlike other cats, jaguars kill
with a bite to the head.

When he takes you by the hand,
it's an invitation to go
to where you have always
had an invitation to go –

Where Light's canine teeth
pierce
the Darkness.

It is here where wounds become
Sacred Wounds.

It is here where artists make vows to beauty,
musicians become composers,
poets transform poems into prayers,
prayers become a way of walking,
and the body begins to understand Love.

It is here where poison becomes Medicine.

Follow this path,
this Path,
though it twists and turns sharply downward,
though it leads to the lair
of everything you have been avoiding...

for a long, long time.

Follow *this* Path,
though you realize:

You've already been here.

This is the cave of your Dreams.

Yes, yes!

All those nightmares were
perfectly inscribed love notes
from the lily-scented Underworld,
always beckoning you to claim the
potential of this place,

Calling on you to honor
your blood –

The red thread embroidering
the edges of the tapestry
in which past, present, and future
are continuously being
woven together
in a circle.

Back to the jaguar:

I have found him to be a trusty guide.

And, odd as it may seem,

Thanked him for the bite.

THE MESSAGE
Buddy's Poem

Can we be here without a purpose?
I don't think we can. Earth is too
wise to waste herself on us.

A wound can come and set us
upon a path; the big ones do.

Stepping stone: Learn humility from scars.

Stepping stone: Apprentice to imperfection.

Stepping stone: Claim the beauty of your soul.

Yes, I do believe in traveling this way.

Once I met a high-spirited eagle with
a crooked yellow beak who had been
grounded for life
by the infectious bite of a tiny mosquito.

You'd think that humiliating
for such a bird,

enraging.

But no,

this bird tossed a stone in front of me,

arched his head back

and screamed into the heavens,

"Compassion!"

And, I knew, absolutely knew,
in that moment
he meant

for everything.

THE OPPOSSUM IN THE ROAD

My father returned earlier than expected
from his Saturday afternoon motorcycle ride.

"There's a mother 'possum and babies
dead in the road," he said.

"Do you want to see it?"

I was a tom boy of, perhaps, ten.

And, I wasn't going to miss this.

I reached for the extra helmet,
shiny blue,
lined with thick black foam,
and snugged it down over my long pig tails.

Chin strap.

Off we went on his orange Honda.

Our destination was what would have
been considered a country road back then.

I remember the temperament
of the sun on my bare arms
and the way my body swayed,
left then right,
adjusting for the curves.

Decades later,

I can still kneel there.

And touch.

And be touched.

I couldn't tell if she'd almost
succeeded,
or barely started;

It didn't matter.

She lay on her right side.
The eyes were open, dull, void of spirit.

The mouth agape in a manner
suggesting a last hiss at oncoming rubber.
The legs protruded, outstretched and stiff.

Yes. She was dead. Not playing dead.

"What interesting feet," I thought.

And I recalled the tracks I'd seen in books –
How they matched these funny
multi-directional pads and toes. All pink.

Under my fingers the long thick tail
felt dry and rather scaly – almost reptilian.

Years later I would learn
that opossum ancestors
hung out with dinosaurs.

I caressed her – this dead mother.

Greys and whites and blacks.
Hairs of different lengths
and stiffnesses
and softnesses;
The short dingy ones on her
long, narrow face
would never be cleaned of
mud spat and road debris.

And long whiskers: three sets.
Eye brow whiskers and cheek whiskers
and whiskers on either side
of a bloody, scraped up nose.

I wondered:

"What does this world
smell like
to an opossum?"

I wanted to be a 'possum,
smelling the world.

Whiffff. Whiffff.

Regretfully,

I can't remember what that
particular day smelled like to me;
My body has forgotten how
to be that kind of animal.

But I do remember the number eight.

There were eight babies,

miniatures of their mother,
all the size of my young hand.

And they hadn't died instantly,
at least, not all of them.

I deducted this on that asphalt
in the glare of my late afternoon initiation:
They had crawled,
one tiny odd little foot at a time,
onto her sky-facing side and
slumped there, gripping their abandonment.
So short their lives.

Did I suddenly understand innocence?

Quietly,

I concluded that there
were some words that I would
have to grow into.

⁓

As a child, I knew the sacred
in ways that it can be hard for
an adult to remember.

It was simply, there.
And, here.

And thus, I had saved wonderment
of her mysterious underbelly pouch
for last.

Marsupial.

Marsupium. Latin.

1. An external pouch or fold on the abdomen
of most female marsupials, containing the
mammary glands and in which the young continue
to develop after leaving the uterus.
2. A temporary egg pouch in various crustaceans and fish.

Pouch. Old English.

1. A small bag for carrying loose items in one's pocket.
2. A sack or bag for carrying mail or diplomatic dispatches.
3. A leather bag or case for carrying ammunition.
4. A sealed container for packaging food.
5. Something resembling a bag in shape.
6. A saclike structure, such as the external abdominal pocket
in which female marsupials carry their young.

Sacred feminine. Origin Unknown.

Undefined.

My body knew what I suddenly understood.

But I didn't have the language for it.

⁓

When I did stand up again,
it was to survey the road.

Up and down.
This way and that.

Had they tried to stop?

I wondered.

I wanted to know.

Had they tried to stop?

What would it have taken to stop?

—

We are the driver.

We are the opossum.

We are the future generations.

What will it take for us to stop?

—

Tonight I stopped what I'd been doing.

(Which was writing this poem)

And walked out the back door
to listen to the sounds of the night.

A young opossum was there,
right there,
on the other side
of the threshold,

awaiting me.

The woman I've become.

I wasn't going to miss this.

So, we sat together for an hour.
In meditation.

Just the two of us

and every voice
in the darkness.

And you know what ...

They were all asking the same question.

It was the very same question asked of me
more than thirty years ago
on a curvy country road
when my eyes first fell on that dead Mother.

Come to your knees.

They asked:

"What will it take for you to come to your knees?"

And, suddenly, I found a word.

~

Mercy.

TURTLES

They've figured this out,
clearly – see how time chooses
the wise – what it is to know the
fleshy body as home – to inhabit this place
that so many fear to claim with the name they've been given.
And notice how peaceful one can then become,
though, yes, there are exceptions.
Was it patience?
Was it perseverance?

Let the thin veneer of moss grow slick and
rings hint-gossip of life story in the scutes of
her carapace as she strides,
slowly, between some place and
somewhere else, maybe a tawny mushroom patch;
it is of no great nerosis to her, or me.

I know she is out ahead of us, this one.

I – standing here beside her –

I am praying that someday,

some day,

we'll be able to catch up.

THE VOW

This that we do with our lives
is a vow,

a promise,

a service if we go at it
humbly enough.

When its golden eyes and gills
become parched in the biting air
and its gaze knows nothing
more than what a hungry
bear can offer of itself,

it is done.

There is nothing more to do.

It is this.

There is no other reason for
any of us to struggle our way
into this world as we do.

All our lives we are called:

"Come!"

"Come!"

We hear.

"This way!"

We call it longing because
we have forgotten
that we speak the usual
language of wild things.

Yet, up river we go.

We must.

We must yield.

Yes.

This we do with our lives
is a vow,

an agreement made in secret
with something truly holy,

a sacrament.

Yes.

I'll tell you how I know:

I watched a sockeye salmon die.

And, for the first time,

I really understood

my life.

FREEING THE WILD

AT THE HEART OF THE MEADOW

Don't stop on the edge of the meadow.
You cannot take the pulse of the
wildflowers from there.

Intimacy is at the core of all things.
You must get thickly into it.
You must lay your fears down
at the threshold
if you hope to release the small
of your back into the cradle
of whatever it is you love.

And look up at the sky.
Or let gravity pull you into another.

I have known what a day is like
without ecstasy,
what a night is like when the
loneliness you keep in empty company
fills you so full of void that
you can't hear
the stars singing.

Such moments were not intended
for anything that breathes.

If the long grasses sliver the length
of your legs, say:

"I am wounded,"

but do not make an event of it.

Instead, look back at what
you have
trampled upon
and offer apologies
in the form of lavish praise.

It is the beauty that you see
there that will turn
your scars
into skin so sensitive
that it longs for
touch from the living.

I once saw a doe come to
nurse her newborn fawn
in the white-blossomed
rose thickets.

She knew to place that which
was most precious
at the heart of the meadow,
and to nurture it there.

Why would she have done
anything less
if she could do this?

And I can do it too.

When the indigo bunting sings,

"Sweet, sweetie, sweet,"

I wonder if you'll meet me there.

BEETLES

Perhaps they are here to teach us humility,
And that is what so many people
find disturbing about their six legs

And hard casing, and the way they crawl
and fly – Sometimes under the yellowy porch lights
at night. Sometimes in the thick garden. What they read
with antennae, I know, our world-lonely bodies
could never know. This I grasp at as an ache.

They need not adorn themselves. I suspect
the thought of doing so would never cross their
little minds. Why bother? They are the living jewels
sculpted by the very same jeweler we deny,
that we will not give ourselves over to.

We can't count them. We can't name them. Not all of them.
And in this is evidence of our lack of desire for
true intimacy with the living.

We wish to remain strangers from the multitudes.

You cannot convince me otherwise; everywhere you can see
how the backs are turned.

What is this great fear of finding out who we
are through relationship with another?

I think that I must admit this:

I have a love for the stars that course the heavens,
And at least an equal love for the beetles of this earthly plane.

If I can do but one thing and one thing only with
the time I have remaining,

it is to bow my head

and open my heart

to this —

an inordinate fondness for life.

BREAK FREE

How we need to be free!

I watch the butterflies emerging from their chrysalises,
folded and fat-bodied with amazement,

"What are these?!"

and the damsels, stepping out of their cellophane-like
exoskeletons like elegant ladies exiting a tattered
carriage for a long anticipated gala.

In the soft-lined cups hidden within
the rose and blackberry brambles,
naked little beaked-things are cracking
their way out of perfect eggs
and finding their "feed me, World!" voice.

The bluebells have once again pushed through
the hard red clay and molding leaf litter
to make offerings of delightfully nodding flowers, which

bees newly emerged from comb cells visit for a spell.

While, at the pond, a bronze-colored froglet
walks onto dry land and experiments with hopping.

Do you know this kind of satisfaction —

The kind that can only come from whole-bodied emergence?

This, I believe, is what is impatiently awaiting you.

Spring, in every which way, is repeating two words:

Break. Free.

AKHILANDESHVARI'S CROCODILE

Sometimes it seems like
your entire world is
in a tail spin.

Everything moves so fast that
focus and certainty
become nothing more than the
theoretical constructs

you obligingly recount
in stories wailed to your old self
with a sense of foolish piety.

Welcome aboard.

You're riding the scaly back
of Akhilandeshvari's crocodile.

Around and around you go.

Weeeeee!

Let's See:

How many pieces have you broken into?

Count them.

There's a pretty good chance
that the head has been severed
at the neck

and the heart has been
sliced open.

"Cosmic surgery!"
gleefully shout the mystics
in all the Truth traditions.

"Spinning,
when invoked with courageous intent,
can nourish the body and soul,"
they say.

Have you not noticed
the feverish whirl
of their dance,
instruments,
and tongues?

Torn apart from the masks,
self betrayals,
and toxic aphrodisiacs
in all forms and strides,

Your inventory will reveal that
all that no longer serves
has been purged from your
own reptilian being.

It is impossible for you
to reconstruct
what was.

Yeah!

Congratulations –
you've had a complete break down.

The dark ferryman will help you
disembark from the crocodile
at the next bridge crossing.

When he does,
look for the sign.

It will read something like this:

"Only you know the way."

Oh, and re-member to thank
the crocodile.

If you look closely,
you'll catch a glimpse
of your indestructible beauty
reflected in his tears.

Akhilandeshvari is known as the Goddess of Never-Not-Broken.

THE CRAYFISH

Grow

Out of the hardness,
tough parts,
that which keeps you small,

The boundary between
the beating heart and
the rhythm of all
else.

Shed your skin,
the exoskeleton,
the structure that
defined you
to the world.

Expose the softness.
Be raw and tender.

Between one you
and the next is
vulnerability,
yes,
and the ego's lament.

To keep growing is
to risk being
on the way to everything
or nothing at all.

There are choices -
a rock
or a heron's feet.

Choices,
the outcome of
which is Destiny.

EMERGENCE

It is time.

Crawl up from the underworld.
Depart your long stay in
thick darkness and clay.

Find your roots.

Find your roots.

Follow – straight or
spiraling – to the surface and
into the humid,
star-storied night.

Proceed slowly, yes,
but with the unyielding intent
to become the amazing thing
that you have never before
seen.

Can you feel your soft, tender body
up against the inside of your
dry, tight skin?

The edge. The tightness.

It tears you apart...

this back-splitting longing to
be larger than that which has
contained you.

I know that dream.

The one about having wings.

So, find that place where you will,
consciously,
take the last step as who you have been,
unfold your future,
and cast the old story behind you.

Emerge. Break free.

Surrender to your destiny,
lifting your long struggled form forth
onto a tree truck,
or a flower stalk.

The moistness.
It is always there –
conception, growth,
birth, life, death.

Notice the eyes.

Red.

Let the soft dawning breezes
caress your sensitive nature,
as you unfurl lacy,
iridescent dreams.
So clear.

Now firm in the daylight.
You are seen.

Listen.

The world is calling to you.

Let yourself be heard.

Trust in what you have been
gifted.

Trust in what you have been
gifted.

Take flight –

with this core truth:

Where you land
and what you do
will determine
how well grounded
we are in the future.

HERMIT THRUSHES IN THE MORNING

On an overcast morning in July,
hermit thrushes
ping-pong snippets of their
liquid melody between
north and south ridges.

I don't understand
the loquacious banter
and I think this tragic.

If a pair of angels stood
in my midst,
would I just carry on,
neglecting to surrender my being
to the symphony of their
holy language?

Intimacy is the turnkey to the soul.

Unbearable passion is what births
everyday miracles.

Why choose to explain a cloud
rather than lie on your back
in tall grasses
and watch a menagerie
shapeshift as it passes?

I don't claim to have any answers,

But I know this world wasn't made
to entertain the diminutive thoughts
of reasonable people.

This world was made for those
whose heart breaks
for want of a grand romance
in which they can
never fully partake.

THE INSISTENT MOTH

Why do you insist
on the long beaten path
of suffering, and
sacrificing your glory-winged being
to the light?

You are of no service
crumpled under a lamp shade
or singed at candle toe.

Do you not know that
there is a lucid holiness
to be had in
the dark abyss?

Reject not the black heavens.

You have caterpillared
and cocooned.
Though death to form
may seem like a way of life,

This time the stars are
counciling you
to Live.

Oh my love,
what would it take
to extend your heart
and flutter your soul
while in the cup of
my gentle hands?

Out the door.

I have faith –
When no longer an addict
of self-flagellation,

The Light that craves You
will enlighten within.

THE MARK

At first I wanted to hide them
from the hunters;
These four tawny brown,
horizontal slashes
with their shreds and peels of
old black birch bark
in which a late-wandering
black bear had written,

"I am here!"

I often keep secrets of the
forest folk,
especially this time of year.

"Shhhhhh!" I wanted to say.

"Shhhhh! These people,
drunk on sorrows
and looking for retaliation for
wounds you didn't place,
seek to kill you.

These people have forgotten
the proper way
to take medicine."

But when the rust-gnarled
pickup approached,
thundering down the mountain
slope, throwing twisting red
dust clouds
into the chilled air,

I stepped beside the tree,

and stood, plainly,
at the edge of the road.

You see:

In a split second, I had re-membered
what it is to be human.

You see:

In each one of us
is a deep desire
to leave a mark.

You see:

The one true mark you are
uniquely here to leave
necessitates that you risk
your life in being seen.

The courageous and
the sacred fools
make their mark anyway.

They make their mark anyway
because choosing to be
vulnerable
is our human medicine.

I smiled and waved to these
strangers on the Ridge.

You see:

I wanted to let them know
that they'd been fully seen.

MEANINGFUL RELATIONSHIP

The dew-dampened swallowtail
braves her first flight of the day,
heavy with night on her wings
but compelled to risk everything
for voices calling out to her to nectar
them into service.

We can't do this alone,
this gifting of ourselves,

this making meaning of our
our embodiment.

Everything is longing for you to give
it purpose through relationship.

Inhale plant.
Exhale animal.
Inhale plant.
Exhale animal...

The ochre-colored grasshopper
half-floating, half-sunk
in the water bucket
showered my hand with dainty kisses
when I lifted him, dripping,
and kept him company in the sun
until he could cast into the
grasses and strum.

Today, it was our task
to love each other.

Tomorrow, the birds will sing
for me as I leave them
an offering of striped
sunflower gratitude.

The toad will wink at me
with his left golden-orb
and puff his heavenly body
when I pass him on the
muddied trail,

saying, "Hello Handsome."

There is no end to the possibilities
of what we could do for each other.

Sit with that for a spell.

～

"How can I help?"

With these four words,
you can live
the meaning of life.

With these four words,

we can make a world.

THE NIGHTINGALE

The nightingale presses her
soft feathered breast
into the spike of the thorn,

penetrating her own aching heart
as her song dies
at sunset.

Or does she?

What if, instead,

The nightingale melods her
melancholy into the world's
most lovely verse,

so strong and convincing
in the depth of its sincerity
that the rose sheds its thorns
into the previous season's
leaf litter and raises its
most fragrant blossomed branch
skyward, as a thrown
for her to perch upon
as she sings her heart outward
at sunset?

Self-inflicted wounds
are an option,

so too is the courage to
feed pain as a holy sacrament
to Truth and Beauty.

Only the latter speaks to Love.

I know birds well enough
to believe the nightingale's
song emerged from swallowing
whole the ancient sorrows
of the wounded feminine,

gestating them around the
turns of the Great Spiral,

and gifting them back to the
world in new-born form.

This is not lost power,

but forgotten power.

Well, not completely forgotten.

Within you there is a nightingale
and there is a rose bush,

you've been referring to them
as all the things that you long
to manifest,

but have been afraid to deserve
because a woman
you respected once showed
you how to lean into thorns

and you believed that's how
it had to be,

always.

This poem is here to say:

"That's not true."

These words are a song that
came to me on the rose-scented
breeze,

one evening,

at sunset,

carried in a voice that my blood knew

as kin.

It was the sound produced across the
lactating vocal chords
of Remembering Woman,

re-membering.

Re-membering to me her primal ties
to the innate courage
to embody Life.

For so many generations we have
been dying away
at our own hands.

It's time to step clear of
the thorns,

isn't it?

You've been sensing this too,

I know.

When Remembering Woman asked
me what she could do to help,

I asked for my own song,

a song likened
to the nightingale's most lovely
sunset song.

I was absolutely sure this would do it.

She said to me,

"You've been singing it
all along, Dear Girl."

"Oh?" I replied.

"Yes," she went on.

"But now you must believe in
what you sing.

That's the difference between
being a girl and being a woman.

The girl knows the words.

The woman knows within her
what they mean."

And, so, at sunrise,
that's the choice I made,

to admit that I know what my
own song means.

The rose bush blushed when
it heard me say it out loud.

I figure that's a very good
place to start.

THE ORIOLE BY THE RIVER

The oriole chortling by the river
is so much more than simply a bird
glimpsed in the bush.

It is a never-again moment
witnessed,
and shared.

How can I not but feel split open?

I am an innocent,
but one who has willfully surrendered
my heart to Life's intent to grow
each one of us into something
larger than the body can contain.

In saying — "Yes!" — to whatever this
is,
I have invited my own undoing.

Anything that has emerged from an
egg,
a seed,
a cocoon,
or a mother's womb

knows the awe-full process of
breaking from confinement.

What pain.

What ecstasy.

Destiny lies in the way we view

the world when we first open our eyes.
We are so small in the context
of this big and bold and expansive
universe of possibility...

Question 1:

Will you succumb to fear,
crawling back into homespun captivity?

Or...

Question 2:

Will you choose to fully emerge,
embracing vulnerability as your savior?

I can't help but wonder what that bird
thought when it first peered,
naked,
beyond the confines of its edgy nest cup.

Reflecting upon a moment
by a river,

I have such gratitude for its wings.

A RABBIT IN THE PORCHLIGHT

There in the newly mown grass
in the shadow cast by freshly lit porch light,
something, something simple has put itself there as
a reminder that we are not alone.
Big brown eyes.
It is cordial, perhaps,
beautiful and non-threatening,
chewing on clover and listening for whatever
it is the arriving night wants to say;
things that we cannot dare imagine because we have
forgotten the value of trying to hear and
be heard – though our survival used to depend
on it – well, actually, it still does –
and so here I am in awe of little things,
simple little things, that haven't forgotten
themselves, nor given up hope for our souls.
What do I do when I realize the rabbit feasting
at dusk understands things that I fear
well enough to expose himself in spite of them?
Certainly, I could learn, couldn't I?
And there he goes, hopping,
moving deeper into the darkness
where life or death awaits.
He's listening for it,
I know,
but he doesn't stop his vigil with himself.
So maybe I could soften,
maybe I could,
and move a little further away from the light.

Vulnerability:
flight, fight, or freeze.

Haven't we been here long enough to find
a better way?

I could turn the porch light off,
and step into the warm summer air,
and undress,
and listen with the pricked hairs of my body
to whatever is out there,

whatever wants to come close.

The switch is greyed by finger prints.
The door knob is round and cold.
The hinges, creak.

Certainly,

I must
take the risk
to open.

SOUL LINES

How do you know that I am not
your great grandmother
or that one day I will not be
your grandson?

Maybe I have been a camel
and you, a chimpanzee.

If I am ever a bird,
I pray that I am gifted
a far better voice.

They speak of the Seventh Generation –
Our need to protect this land,
these waters,
the air we breath
for them –

the unborn.

What if we are to be the Seventh Generation

come again,

re-birthed?

Am I stealing in this life from
the body that will
carry me in the next?

Two-legged?
Four-legged?
Finned?

I think it would be best if we
were all spiders
at least once.

Perhaps that's what it takes
to understand

how interconnected,

delicate,
and miraculous

the Web.

SUBTLE BEAUTY

I can respect beauty that
screams,

"See me!"

and recognize in it my own
innate desire to be noticed.

Blooming is about attraction,
and attraction is an
investment in everything
that is to unfold.

When I was a little girl,
I'd pick buttercups
because they were the
brightest, cheeriest flowers
in the seldom-mown grass.

That was some time ago.

As a woman,
I am drawn to beauty that
is more subtle,

Beauty that requires you
to really look to see a thing.

Beauty that whispers,

"Know me..."

And seeks to release us from
lingering fears of intimacy.

Today the beauty to which
I apprentice sits atop a
bloated carcass.

So many have called him
ugly and disgusting.

He's been persecuted,
poisoned and shot
for his appearance and habits.

Where we look,

we see aspects of ourselves.

Already the blood has thickened
and the body stiffened,
and he has made the first
strategic tear in the tawny doe skin
that once held a spirit
close to the bones.

I gaze upon every inch of him:

The wrinkling of his bald, black head.
The delicate flare of unencumbered nostrils.
Feathers like pitch.
Scaled feet that remember the ancient
bloodlines and know that their place
is below broad, powerful wings.

His crop bulges, but he is not afraid
to be satiated,
and will join with others of his kind
to pick a body clean;

Sharp, nimble beaks and time
have enabled vultures to swallow
what others cannot.

And this is how it goes in these old fields:

This subtle beauty,

This dark angel on a mission,

escorting the dead,
piece by piece,
nutrient by nutrient,
into the ground
where all former lives
become caretakers of the living.

And this, to me, is beautiful.

Yes, it is true, I have found beauty

and, yes, of course, I shall go on looking for it.

I shall seek out beauty in all
the still hidden places,

All those places I have yet to
dare to go.

Though, yes, in truth,

I do already know:

It is there.

It is always there.

WHOOO

Tonight the barred owls
ask their question upon
the chill of dusk;

one from the tulip poplar grove,
the other at creekside.

"Whooo?"

Is what they want to know.

"Whooo?"

It's a dangerous inquiry.

A warrior's initiation right
if you dare seek the answer.

Do you dare?

Do you dare to know
who you truly are?

Coyotes run the crest of the ridge,
yips and howls
formulating the collective voice
of the pack.

Don't listen to them,

they are tricksters.

This is what I have to say:

If you go searching for the
answer,

you will Die.

And if you don't go searching
for the answer,

you will die.

If you want to Live,

you *must* go searching
for the answer.

The moon will light the way in the darkness,
but only so much as to allow
you to take one uncertain step
at a time,

often, backwards.

You'll find that what the sun illuminates,
is frequently outsized by its
shadow,

and that the shadow has a life of its own.

You are going to have to
befriend it,
as your fellow journeyman.

Be prepared to leave who you
think you are behind

in the quest for
authenticity.

It's best if you put down the large bundle
of "what no longer serves"
at the trail head.

Do bring your most spectacular heartaches
and your deepest wounds;
these are the trail markers that
will help you stay on course.

And too, have within you
a most
beautiful verse.

You cannot fully understand who you
are until you have courted the
Beloved with such wild abandon,
that you become completely undone.

"Whooo?"

from the top of the tallest pine.

"Whooo?"

from the sycamore at the edge of the meadow.

"Who?"

from the moment you were born,

has been the question

gifted by those who

want you to find your way

Home.

THE WINTER WREN

How can a little brown bird flit
across your path,
yet remain perched as a precious haunt
in your psyche for days?

The winter wren is a secret
come out from the thick greenbrier
to look you in the eye
and let you know only
that it has suddenly revealed
itself in the brisk, dancing
air.

What secret?

This bird took no measure
to say.

How often aspects of us
show up without announcement
or explanation,

flitting into our awareness
with the hope that we will
See.

We are more mystery to
ourselves than we know.

The sky can't decide
on blue or gray,
and the clouds are directionally
fickle

as I ponder the winter wren
hop-skipping through
my dense woodland.

"What is it you want of me?"
I ask.

"It's a secret,"
is the only reply.

And this is what I concluded:

I can love what I do not know.

Countless bodies are breathing
in windswept thickets
around me,
and without me knowing of them,
or them of me,
we are entwined and my heart holds
inexplicable space for them.

What is yet unrevealed of me, too,
is lovable.

LIVING WILD

ANSWERS FOR MARY

Yes!
I saw it, its bill like the compass needle
which is wholly committed to truth.
I knew of its pertinence the very moment
my heart took flight.
You see, beauty isn't for figuring.
Beauty exists only for the embodiment of beauty —
a holy union of form and essence
to be lived into the world like
the sacred contract between mated swans.
And oh yes,
with this,
I've changed my life.

Response to questions asked by Mary Oliver in her poem, *The Swan*.

THE EAGLET

What if your nest
was a cathedral?

And, why isn't it?

We all yearn for sanctuary
under the same tempest
skies.

Here I feel I should humbly
and somewhat awkwardly
confess,

I am human.

What would you think of that?

I wonder.

Do other species feel the
need to apologize for
inhabiting their own skin?

What has humanity granted
either one of us?

Thank you.

I have the answer in the way
you look at me:

"This moment," you say.

"This moment."

And it's true.

It is in this moment that
we get to decide
who and what
we want
to be.

It's always in 'this moment.'

The red mud feels cold and wet
as it hugs my right knee.
This I can do to honor you,

because I am human.

EASTERN BLUEBIRDS AND PURPLE SPIDERWORTS

The purple spiderworts showed up
on her last walk in the mountains –

Their long, dark green leaves
bending and flowing,
their deep violet, three-petalled
flowers wide open to a sun
whose canopy-filtered light
was prancing about the forest floor.

I remember it:

How she "ooed" and "ahed"
over these small, docile plants.

How they captivated her like
nothing else had that day.

How they weren't going to
let her go.

So, her old friend said:

"Well head back to the barn, fetch a shovel.
You can take some home, plant them in your garden."

None of us spoke about the things
the gesture presupposed,
though we all knew.

Yes. We knew.

The bluebirds showed up the
Spring before –
flitting about the patch of tall
grasses that she could
see from her bedroom window.

Everything about them
was oh so very cheery
and charming.

Though she'd never
especially delighted in birds,
she delighted in these –

Little feathered sprites
flashing vibrant colors
and repeating "tu-a-wees."

They amused,
and distracted,

carrying away time,

and other things
not spoken of.

An old wooden chair
was installed by the window
and a brand new nesting box
on a post – straight and tall.

They were roosting places,

for awhile.

Do we have a choice in what claims us?

She became bluebirds
and spiderworts.

Why these?

Why not lilies, or a particular rose?

Why not the nestling rabbits
she had tried to save from a
marauding dog?

For eighteen Springs,
I've quietly peeked in
to count the bluebird eggs

one
two
three
four
five

and come to my knees
to tend these very same
spiderworts.

I've sat in the cemetery,
wondering:

When my time comes,
will I have been claimed?

And, if so,
will I know what has claimed me?

Will I have any clue,
given all the grand possibilities,
what it is that wants to keep
repeating my name?

Will I somehow know what is to become of me?

And,
most importantly,
will I have time enough

to speak of it?

Will I have time enough
to say,

"Thank you,"

through some yet-to-be-determined

gesture of gratitude?

FAWN

Is any human heart
naïve to the texture of
abandonment?

Here I am snugged in
tall grasses and sunspots,

Still but for my newly-boned rib cage
and the short-bodied flowers
that play flower games in exhalations.

I could be here all day;
What joy there is in bird song,
and the tremendous leap of
shiny
green
grasshoppers,
and soil – how it smells.

I am of this place
and its daily-recounted secrets.

I ask you:

"Please don't save me."

I am busily laying in this meadow,

saving you.

FINCHES IN THE MORNING

At the feeders,
in the brisk of morning air,
they come
golden and fluffed
miniatures of the one sun
that everything is waiting for.

Finches cracking the hard shelled seeds
of flowers that radiated their own
kind of celestial joy during a summer
now passed into bittersweet memory.

In the lingering grey of this frigid dawn,
I ask the steam rising from
the kettle:

Do they long for the months
behind and ahead?

Do they count days until they
are once again swaying
like brilliant pendulums on man-tall
flower stalks?

Or, perhaps, they know every moment
as its own kind of happiness:

The look of the black and white stripes.
The width and weight.
The bulbous triangular shape.
The crackle as it breaks.
How far the shards fall and where.
The taste of the tender kernel bits.

The long streak of darkness that flies
so swiftly with equal awareness and intent
from the patient cover of cedar bough.

The air-piercing blades seeking
to grasp the small butter-faced flash
of feathers and flesh

that is now deep in the boxwoods
because it knew precisely
how and when
to change its focus and perch.

And I was there,
at the window,
loving this world,

Making no mistake in judging
the outcome;
each having needs
and a gift of service to
offer through their living,
and dying.

And me, and you?
Could we want anything more?
Could every moment matter this much?

FREEZE AND THAW

There are frog eggs and there is snow.
This, to me, is wonderful.
I live in a place where frogs,
entire little brown frogs,
freeze and thaw!

I think this spectacular.

I think this is spectacular,
in part,
because I find it humbling.

I like it when my practice of
worship entails coming
to my knees for a closer look.

And there is ice on the vernal pool.

Except in one spot.

It's the spot where the frogs
collectively laid their eggs before the
temperatures plummeted
and the storm came.

Before the storm came!

How did they know the sun
would favor that particular
two by two foot spread for
wetness above all others?

How did they know?

Alternate hypothesis # 1:

There is a heat-generating relationship
between the gelatinous egg masses
and solar radiation playing out before
my eyes, on this air-chilled day,
in ways I cannot see.

Alternate hypothesis # 2:

It is both:

Long time-selected forethought
and engineering.

Alternate hypothesis # 3:

It's a miracle.

Today, I'm not inclined to choose.

Rumor has it that it will be in
the 60s again on Sunday.

That's two days away.

The frogs will thaw.

I will ask.

IN THIS WAY

The pudgy voles must be
nestled deeper now,
the meadow grasses damp
with the weeping of
half-hearted snow flurries,

And the fox and owl
tucked in by morning light,
stomachs robust and satiated
or burning with a hunger
strong enough to feed fear
into the hours ahead.

This is how I awaken.

Life on earth is a written language
that is read through the
living of it.

What is most tempting of
this day is everything that
I don't know about its
unfolding.

My Beloved is like this,
fully present yet always
out of reach of anything
intent on the possession
of answers that would shorten
the moment's extended hand.

To be betrothed to
the Great Mystery
is to say "yes" to everything

that cannot be planned:

The next breath,

The next lover,

Death,

And how each will
take you in their arms,

with, or without,
mercy.

The vole knows only the
last pinch of the talon,
and the tongue-pressing
swallow of the fox,

but even in this,
there is time enough to
breathe out these words,

"So that was my life.

I am so very grateful."

And in passing this way,
so many times,
you place your own
punctuation marks
in the Great Story,

Stops,
starts,
and the kind of exclamations

that can only come
from embodied feeling.

In this way,

You live and die,

in the way all
exhausted
lovers do.

IRRATIONAL OPTIMISM

I am a nestling eastern phoebe
perched upon the edge
of the moss-lined mud cup
that is the only home I've ever known.

Here, under the roof eves
of the tattered house,
sixteen days have passed
since my egg-tooth
sliced open a world of possibility.

I have grown large in my dreaming
and this womb-bowl too small –

Feted on juicy vain insects,
my plump pin-feathered siblings
and I hunger for
more.

The sky is large and come-hither blue.

I know nothing of the experience
of flight,
but it consumes my definition
of self in entirety.

The distance between here
and the nearest tree is great.

The distance between here
and the rock-hard ground is great.

There are four cats below.
Three of them have been calculating.

I am on the edge.

I am the embodiment of
irrational optimism.

—

And I am flying.

OWL

In the arc of my wings,
the amber of my eyes,
the lucid throttle of my talons,
I am built to hold you,

In sacred silence.

How do you choose
to hold
me?

RED FOX

Darkness is the cape that
clothes me.

I am learning to see with
listening eyes,
and walk silently amidst the
shadows.

Edges are pathways,
not boundaries.

Beyond the edge is openness.

To play there is to risk death.

By the light of the moon, I play,
letting my vippy voice carry
what could be my last moment into the wind.

What secret is nestled in the
leaves?

RISING

Paddling upward through layers of sand
with no knowledge of where to,
crazed, or mightily faithful,
I don't know and I refuse to judge
these hundreds of tiny flippers
in a frenzy to meet the Great Mystery,
and possibly their death, imminently.
I prefer to crouch here in awe.
What they don't know, I know:
Ghost crabs, raccoons, birds, big birds,
fish, big fish. They, many of these
little naïve ancient ones, will be snacked upon
like salted popcorn. Nab, swallow, and gone
from this world they barely entered
and could not name.
Look how they rush to their destiny,
risking everything because that's
what it is to live, though, yes, that's the terrible secret
that we keep shushing back into the underworld,
and look how they, bellies skidding, go forward to reach
the one world they are made for, and how,
like an equal lover, that world, that mighty crashing world,
is reaching back to them in waves. And, they are met.

Gasp.

Isn't this what you want?
The perfect fit. The equal lover.

These precious scrambling things have got it right.
Standing in the sea oat-waving dunes, I'm absolutely sure of it.

How can the body, this body, any body
refuse to take the risk to rise?

SACRAMENTS

How does last night's fallen snow
feel about the morning sun's radiant touch?

Is there a deep yearning to be melted,
or is there a great fear of death?

I whisper:

"They can be one, the same."

The sharp-shinned hawk throws himself,
like Cupid's hell-bent arrow,
head on into the bough-damp cedars.

He has faith in a universal memory
that has never occupied him personally.

"There will be nourishment at the core of
this dark and tangled thicket."

And he is correct,

Emerging with brown, floppy-necked sparrow
in his blood-warmed talons.

He makes no apology for taking a life
to secure his own,

But he does pull each of the sparrow's feathers
and set them fluttering free into the blue of sky
as his particular way
of making an offering to the Holy.

And is this what it's all about? I wonder:

Every act of life, a sacrament.

SONG FOR THE REINDEER

I owe you my life.
No man can become a man
without otherness.

You are other.
And, you are me.

We are of the same
hoof and bone.

When I consume your body,
you are the knife and the spoon
and the tongue of the ancestors.

How otherwise starved and naked I would be.

Cradle and sled,

You've born me
into this world
and across the miles
that no one else cared witness.

My stride is a learned migration
into my self.

Only here can I know flight.

I may be the breath,
But you are the sound of my soul:

This soft rhythm of the taiga.
These branches snapping in the wind.
The keepers drumming at the threshold

of the world
in which we are true brothers.

Blood lines. Life lines.

There is only one world.

And, this music.

Yes, this music —

I've come to understand
is a Man's initiation.

How could I be without you?

How could I ever be without
you?

SWERVING TO MISS CATERPILLARS

In the Autumn,
when thirteen-segments,
fat and bristled,
dare the frenetic roads to find
tall, dry grasses in which to sleep
themselves into something
utterly different,

caterpillars can be your prayer.

What kind of person do you
choose to be?

Every moment of every day
you have this question put before
you by everything around you.

Everything.

And, everyone.

In that instant in which *you* wake up,
how will
you emerge?

Driving down Route 33,

at this very moment,

I make my choice:

I choose to be the kind of person
who swerves to miss caterpillars.

TADPOLE IN TIRE RUT

Five hundred eighty seven
American toad tadpoles
Anaxyrus americanus,
black as pupils,
swim the shallows
of a tire rut.

Not a single limb bud
promises an impending hop.

The Sun knows this.

I imagine many would scoff
at the foolishness
of the two pudgy, wart-covered
night lovers who swooned
and spawned here
under a naked Moon.

Me?

No. Not me.

I kneel, a student.

Only true masters
have the capacity to
put such faith
in the ephemeral.

THE VITTLES OF DEATH

The broad-winged hawk
raised from the rocky creek bed
with a time-limited garter snake
in her talons.

I knew the bird by the
horizontal white tail barring
and the rapid flap of wing
as she rose toward the emerging canopy veil.

I knew the snake by the
vertical yellow stripes
running the length of body to tail.

They gleamed in the sunlight
stored up by the poplar leaves
for cloudy days
such as this.

What of him was not twisted
and entwined in a mutual
death grip with scaly hawk feet
streamed downward –

though in mid air,
gravity still laying a claim
saying,

"You will return to me."

Perhaps all of us knew gravity
wasn't expecting to see that snake
again in the same configuration
of embodiment.

Most of us were okay with it,
under the circumstances.

So bird and snake got me thinking
about how we living beings
must feed our inner beloved
on the vittles of Death.

Love notes take many forms:

Here my Beloved are the chords of attachment
to beliefs proven too small and inflexible,
to things that constrict and clutter,
and to all those who can only embrace us in pathologies of pain.

Here too I lay down all of the possessions
that ego has acquired through the depletion
of Self and Other.

There are many.

Let me nourish you my Dearest,
tending cellular breath and memory,
on the flesh of animal and plant.
Though I'd like to promise you that every
being came to our lips by choice,
I don't know this to be true.

Our gratitude need be far greater than
Grandmother's mourning.

I kept walking,
knowing somewhere beyond my sight
the extended arm of a large tree on mountain slope
was hosting hawk and serpent
at the shared breakfast table of Gain and Loss.

But before this story was completely over,
I came upon another common garter snake -
this one warming belly in the middle of a winding gravel road.

His tongue flicked in and out,
tasting, sensing.

I said,

"Hello Love,"

and gently moved him out of harm's way.

A WALKING STICK SIGHTING

I met a six-legged walking stick today,
an ochre apparition on late summer
redbud twig.

We sat and talked as the sun
chased its tail in the time-short leaves.

I asked him what he knew about
courting the Beloved.

Without hesitation or bewilderment,
this tiny Master of optical disillusion
replied:

"The eyes don't register
what the heart can't see."

WHAT IS JOY TO THE SNAPPING TURTLE?

What is joy to the snapping turtle?

His beaky jowl open wide
does not invite a kiss.

His algae-slimed carapace
is rough around the edges,
sculpted by millennia of quarrels
with the world.

It does not invoke cuddle, or caress.

Dare you seek his intimate company,
he will hiss, puff, and rise.
Insist, and be met by a strike
of serpentine appearance and precision.

He has no patience for your curiosity,

No want for admiration or allegiance.

Coo and he will think you ridiculous.

When on land,
he has no retreat from your love
and it scares him.

But oh give him the substrate of
pond bottom muck
and all that he has learned
of passion comes alive.

Like a monk who knows
a specific mist-enshrouded mountain
as the extension
of his soul,

the snapping turtle glides
along a thoroughfare of beaver channels
and snacks on lizard's tail plants
as a matter of meditation

and transpersonal expression.

Watch this ancient master long enough
and you will discover what joy is.

Joy is surrendering your entire being
to the element to which you belong.

THE WOODPECKER

The world needs drummers,
And hollow trees
need to speak of the lives
they have lived.

Listen carefully
for the pause,

that faint collection of seconds when the
resistant insect is extracted and swallowed ...

just before the story begins again,

and Death smiles at his own cleverness.

Acknowledgments

Many thanks to Jason Kirkey and L. M. Browning of Hiraeth Press for tending *Wild Life* and releasing it into the world.

To Edward E. Clark Jr., my deepest gratitude for giving a kid a chance, thirty years of friendship, the spirit you bring to this book's foreword, and everything you do on behalf of wildlife.

Numerous friends – known and unknown to me – have supported this book by providing feedback on the poems initially shared through the Talking Waters blog. I am thankful for their audience and all that they have contributed in making this a co-creative project. Two individuals deserve special mention for their ever-present thoughtfulness and encouragement, Richard Heilbrunn and LaRue Owen. Thank you, gentlemen – a deep bow to you.

Muses show up in various forms, often unexpectedly. Sometimes they are direct sources of inspiration, sometimes they invite inspiration, and sometimes their company is inspiring. I am grateful for all of the muses who helped give voice to this collection of poems. These are the ones I can call by name: Eric Lane, Chris Lyal, Masood Arshad Makhdoom, Arne Witt, Christopher Bernetchez, Mary Oliver, Buddy the Bald Eagle, and Buttercup the Black Vulture.

Susan Chernak McElroy, Mare Cromwell, Carolyn Raffensperger, Sean Southey, and Gary Tabor graciously offered *Wild Life* words of praise and endorsement. I am truly honored to know each one of these people – they are champions of the wild. Thank you, friends, for your presence among these pages and your presence in the world.

About the Wildlife Center of Virginia

Each time you purchase a copy of *Wild Life* two dollars will be donated to the Wildlife Center of Virginia.

The Wildlife Center of Virginia exists to provide the highest quality care to native wildlife, often on an emergency basis, as well as to inspire people to become stewards of the natural environment and its inhabitants. Its reach is global.

Since 1982, the Wildlife Center has:

- Treated more than 60,000 wild animals, representing more than 200 species of native birds, mammals, reptiles, and amphibians – from Virginia and beyond.

- Shared the lessons learned from these cases with some 1.5 million school-children and adults.

- Trained a corps of wildlife medicine practitioners, including veterinarians, veterinary technicians, and volunteer wildlife rehabilitators. Those who have benefited from the professional training programs offered by the Center may now be found on the cutting-edge of wildlife veterinary medicine around the world.

In 2007, the Wildlife Center received the National Conservation Achievement Award from the National Wildlife Federation as the Conservation Organization of the Year.

For further information, see: www.wildlifecenter.org

About the Author

Jamie K. Reaser has a deep fondness for the wild, intimate, and unnameable. She received a BS in Field Biology, with a minor in Studio Art, from the College of William and Mary and her doctorate in Biology from Stanford University. She has worked around the world as a conservation biologist, international policy negotiator, environmental educator, and wilderness rites-of-passage guide. She is also a practitioner and teacher of eco-psychology, nature-based spirituality, and various approaches to expanding human consciousness, as well as a poet, writer, artist, and homesteader-in-progress. Jamie has a passion for bringing people into their hearts, inspiring the heartbeat of community, and, ultimately, empowering people to live with a heart-felt dedication to Mother Earth. Her writing explores themes related to Nature and human nature in this magical, yet challenging, time of the Great Turning. She is the editor of the *Courting the Wild* Series, as well as the author of *Huntley Meadows: A Naturalist's Journal in Verse, Note to Self: Poems for Changing the World from the Inside Out* and *Sacred Reciprocity: Courting the Beloved in Everyday Life*. Jamie is a Fellow of the International League of Conservation Writers. She makes her home in the Blue Ridge Mountains of Virginia. Visit her Talking Waters poetry blog at www.talkingwaterspoetry.blogspot.com, or through Talking Waters on Facebook.

ℌIRAETH PRESS

Hiraeth Press is a publisher with a mission.

❡Poetry is the language of the Earth — not just poems but the slow flap of a heron's wings across the sky, the lightning of its beak hunting in the shallow water; autumn leaves and the smooth course of water over stones and gravel. These, as much as poems, communicate the being and meaning of things. Our publications are all poetry, whether they are poems or nonfiction, and reflect the ideal that falling in love with the Earth is nothing short of revolutionary and that through our relationship to wild nature we can birth a more enlightened vision of life for the future. We are passionate about poetry as a means of returning the human voice to the polyphonic chorus of the wild.

www.hiraethpress.com

CPSIA information can be obtained at www.ICGtesting.com
Printed in the USA
BVOW07s2300300713

327379BV00002B/5/P